Winter,
the unwelcome visitor

poems

Shaista Justin

Winter,
the unwelcome visitor
poems

© 2009 Shaista Justin

Except for purposes of review, no part of this
book may be reproduced in any form without
prior permission of the publisher.

We acknowledge the support of the Canada
Council for the Arts for our publishing program.

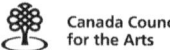 

We also acknowledge support from
the Government of Ontario through the Ontario Arts Council.

Cover image: Thomas Cartwright, *Dozing Turtle Dove in Obz*
Author photo: Veronica Hyatt

Library and Archives Canada Cataloguing in Publication

Justin, Shaista Samreen
    Winter, the unwelcome visitor : poems / Shaista Justin.

ISBN 978-1-894770-52-1

    I. Title.

PS8619.U863W56 2009   C811'.6   C2009-901092-5

Printed in Canada by Coach House Printing

TSAR Publications
P. O. Box 6996, Station A
Toronto, Ontario M5W 1X7
Canada

www.tsarbooks.com

Craig, Keeran, and Julian,
you are worth more than your weight in poetry

Contents

South Africana: On the Way

Winter, the Unwelcome Visitor	1
Table Mountain	3
The Karoo	6
Medulla Oblongata	7
Lambert's Wall	9
Fynbos Fires, Noordhoek, Long Beach	10
Ben in Tamboerskloof	11
On the Way	13
The River Club in Obz	14
The Taxis' Song	15

Post-Colony: Do Not Love Freedom

Do Not Love Freedom	19
Mortar and Steel	21
Immigrant's Tempest	23
My Love is Faithful	25
The Final Menagerie	27
An English Landscape	29
In-Celestial Beginnings	32

Puzzletry   35

Being Brave

Bleeding Coal	39
Lisping Beneath the Cries	41
Being Brave	43
Provoking Sympathy	45

The Lover

The Only Garden	49
Fight the Air	52
Caught in the Cracks	53
Secondary Texts	55
Lindy's Moon	57
Sunshine Dreams and Constellation Plans	59
The Blue-Eyed Dawn	61
Give Way	63

South Africana: On the Way

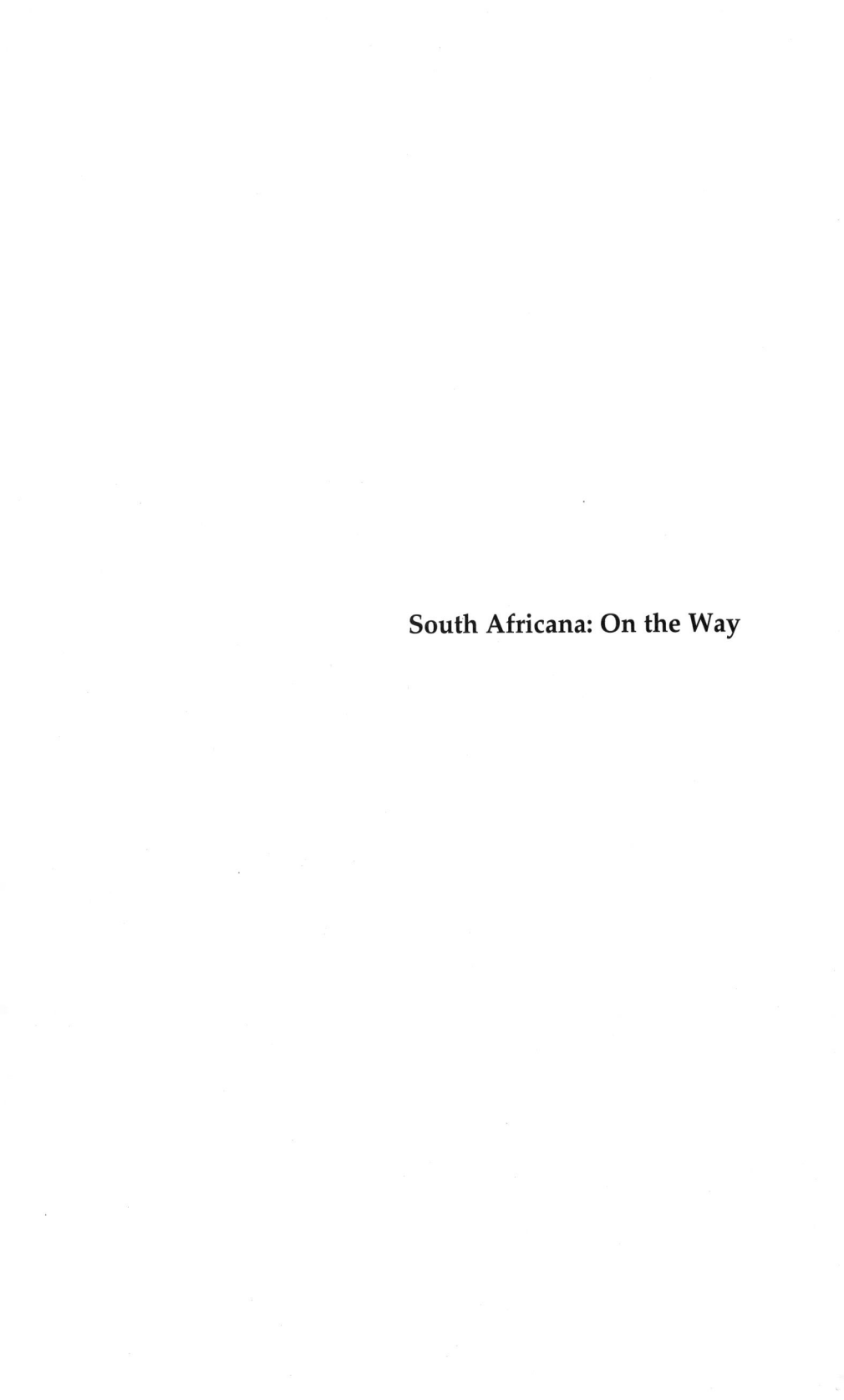

Winter, the Unwelcome Visitor
for CD Laatz

Winter comes like an unwanted visitor
I cannot turn away.

Burning snow pelting me
with a thousand memories,
scalding me with cold.

Go, I say, I wait for African sun,
to be held by a man, a continent away.

*   *   *

But do I regret:

the rain that hails on flooded highways
the biting air that brittles the bones
the wind that breathes your breath astray

the poverty that pursued us
relentless as the vagrants at the door

the summer that sweats in the shade
baking the tin roofs of corroded shacks
hungry light eating the skin away

wandering like lost street children
walking to hope miles delayed

mountains with rocks for foliage
tired shifting of the grey skies
battling with the wearied tides

eyes wide in the darkness
waiting for the murdering thieves to come?

*   *   *

And, I thought I wanted you, Canada.

I remembered you,
like a lonely man recalling a lost love

believing that after all this time
you could still want me
burns and wrinkles, scars and shame

I fantasized about you
like a young girl enchanted with a future to come

But, the golden roads are just asphalt promises;
the welcoming arms are limp and tired;
all hopes and dreams are bogged and mired.

I chafed at my exile
like a refugee aching to return home

to deep forests where I could hide my eyes
night skies as velvet as egg yolks
the winter warming me despite the cold

I remembered a breeze that enlivens each breath;
I remembered a sun that takes forever to set.

What are you to me:
oh husband-less wife, fatherless child,
and pregnant forlorn lover?

Perhaps I do not remember you as you were—

for, the wind tears my cheap coat;
the streetcars scream in clanging ears;
the roaches await their turn in every corner;
as I stare at the snow by the window alone.

*   *   *

I cannot know when he will come;
I watch as the seasons turn me away.

The ocean like a great eye,
in False Bay harbour still staring at the sky.

Table Mountain
for Sylvia Bowerbank and Our Lady Anne

Shadows of jutting rock
false echoes of themselves,
are collapsing in rectangular pieces
of grey and white and red.

A splintered grandeur,
a worn and womb-less grandmother.

Beaten by the sun
or polished by a rag of fog,
the sun breaking on it
or the fog caressing it,

she has surrendered to neither sky nor sea.

The lovely mounds reaching for fullness,
a fecundity unexpectedly flattened,
as though the sky had sat itself down
with an overly ample ass.

Triangles of grass,
entry points to green expanse,
a barren suggestiveness
ending at rock, not pasture.

And then

the sunset, a scarlet rouge,
her visage suddenly made smooth;
when the sun goes suddenly she glows—

She glows,

at the maids lined up
on the Bo Oranjestraat,
brown coats wrapped tight

against more than cold,

like trees on a picturesque avenue
waiting for the taxi home.

She glows,

at the dusty workers
shaking coats and boots
fleet fleeing the monstrous solitude

of the monstrous homes,
returning to a piece of tin
and a bit of fence.

She glows,

at the lonely new mother
catching herself, soothing her
baby, in a window pane

because her husband will not
leave this greater lady, this stranger's place,
this strangling space.

For then,

the harlot's red light fumbling faints
to unveil a stern and ancient virgin
closed and locked up for the night.

No earthly paradise, no nubile soil,
though the sky aches for Caribbean blue,
the sea for tropical warmth.

Though they named the bandy rhino unicorn,
declared the desart a Canaan found,
envisioned cities of the world at her feet,

fruitless trees rest in the lee of a brutal wind.
They are pissing themselves
on hollow oaks that line the president's path.

The travellers have died, starving and aching.

She wraps each one in her cold arms,
staged—not an old maid,
but revealing an old whore after all.

The trees on top of Lion's Head,
as though on pilgrimage,
line-up like dancing elephants
against the sky.

The Karoo

Where warm in winter's cold, the small farms
hide themselves, land wired around;
like sieves which slip in Black arms
shoved tight in bakkies, silently sound.

Medulla Oblongata
(33 Cromer Road, in Cape Town, South Africa.)

The man alone
speaking to himself in the night
in a language outdated, defiled.

Carrying the sound of crickets pulsing time;
the air does not hear him.

He is philosophizing in:
mathematics
nautical notation
and Afrikaans expletives.

Busy hoarding the stars;
the sky does not know him.

He switches into English deciding
that 2cm in any direction offers him
the freedom to walk to anywhere . . .

The mountains cannot feel him;
he does not trouble their slopes with his step.

His problem he proclaims
is -6, which must be *directed by 3 x 4*
feet in opposite directions.

Cradling the roots of green and living things;
the earth cannot touch him.

He cannot find his way home.
He cannot find his way home.
He cannot find his way home.
The streets have trapped him with pavement logic.

His only choice is *blast-off!*

The people do not care for him.
He is drunk.

He is drunk.
He is drunk.

He says:

The earth is spinning on its own axis
in months, the problem of 4 seasons arises—
it must have something to do with the sun

The sun cannot enlighten him:
it has turned its face away.

A car speeds towards him.
Quick!
Quick!
Quick!
You have not time,
he yells.

Following its own compass;
the car barely misses him.

How far is this road allowed
to go in each direction?

He is trapped despite his countdown:
. . . 9, 10,
jump!

But there is no ocean to drown in,
the asphalt has saved him.

Medulla oblongata, I am drunk and stupid,
he exclaims.

The night will continue to keep him:
no streetlight illuminates
no road offers passage
no one comes to lead him
no darkness shows the way.

8

Lambert's Wall

He looks at his painting . . . Actually, everything should
get wings like Angelbee . . . None of them must lie thick
or heavy or flat on the earth. They must fly.
Termite-angel. Angel wasp. Heavenly rats
and moths. Angels for Africa.
    —Marlene van Niekerk, Triomf 283

If the sky with its blue eyes could inhabit
birds with multiple wings,
bees stinging with numerous stingers,
baleful bats seeing with human sight,

then can we not define our own limitlessness
and grow legs on our shoulders
to walk upon the sun,
while it beats us with light shaped like hands?

What monstrous nature will we create,
if left idle to imagine the things that brood
in our laughing hearts.
Can we escape genus and title to tilt
this planet on an unseen axis,

to live on Lambert's wall?

Fynbos Fires, Long Beach, Noordhoek
for Jack

A crippled stand against the ground
the silver leaves burning to death
made golden by the fire
that will bear no lie, no falsehood.

How can we be what we be?

The sun ablaze on the sword of the white sands
the ocean's splayed fingers
throwing themselves on the edge.

Ben in Tamboerskloof

Let us go then, you and I,
When the evening is spread out against the sky
Like a patient etherized upon a table;
Let us go, through certain half-deserted streets;
    —TS Elliot, *The Love Song of J Alfred Prufrock*

You are the letter I dared not write
for fear of bringing home grey slate buildings
the tops of which you photographed incessantly (why?),
stopping me in the half-carved streets
while I toppled on your arm, the cracks in sentiment
becoming obscene, hand clipped back high
hovering between my skin and a plane ticket;
the date of which I could not alter (I did try!) . . .
"Jy is 'n doring", you said, stopped for a monument and sighed.
Let us go then, you and I,

past Gardens, the Gallery, the Nelson, the Labia—
past the tottering of my feet and the strong width
of your breath, and haul my legs up again the incline
of every lost word reclaimed in Tamboerskloof;
where once I claimed the cold air kept me from you
and we sheathed our conversation in Shakespeare by your bed.
Can I linger (this time) and tenderly tinge your eyes
with the nights spent . . . with the wind howling in our sleep
(Did we sleep?), and clasping your wavering hand there we can lie;
When the evening is spread out against the sky.

Then I can write you . . . without remembrance,
with the supple skin of the moment I held your tropes in:
when you screamed the sunlight shining showed
the buildings were blinding like erected snow.
And I know how you wandered those pathways alone
each slitting forth its own assertion of mountains
unable to loose the weight of words tense in your step
words you could not speak (as I could not say your name)
the unrepentant language drugged your tongue disabled,
Like a patient etherized upon a table.

But now when I now no longer weep with every goodbye glance
threatening to drown with the listing of each kiss
where your body became land to my teeth . . . let us leave
the lights of Adderley Street and bend our thoughts tightly
across the misfortune of miles . . . let us open our lips
so I can breathe your eyes blue-cold in African sleet
and take the lost phrases in stride with the memories.
And if you are amongst the ruins of words
then that is where we shall meet (come!);
Let us go, through those certain half-deserted streets.

On the Way
for Nicole

In Hermanus,
where the whales never came,

the land reached out
to greet itself at every curve:
a floss of road
between ochre mountain and salty sea.

They had not time.

Like a tsunami it came at them,
huge, furious, without foresight.
It must have seemed impossible,
a death as relentless as life.

Who could have believed it?

A mother standing bravely,
the last thing I can do for her.
Roadside lilies on a white coffin,
for a child, remarked an old man.

We were to meet, on the way.

Young, Afrikaans girl,
spreading grown-up wings
at an English university,
in an English town.

Forgive me, says a friend,

we were to take her on vacation
far from the sea, away from fate.
She can barely speak, she smiles,
for her family, for her community,

and for her daughter's dark friends from the city.

The River Club in Obz

Mid-winter in Muizenberg,
Oh! Stolen lilacs in June;
Mid-winter in Muizenberg,
Stolen time, stolen so soon.

At the River Club in Obz,

you carry me, arms tight against my spine,
bearing me through the crush of beautiful bodies
as they brush each other, swaying like grass on the veld,
moving to the wind, dancing with arms unfurled.

Carry me away from that awful Norwegian
pressed too close, while the night before
I tried to sleep on the shoulder of the plane.

You don't complain,
that I am too heavy, just press your chest,
think of the wind this dark South African night:
it touches my hair as if it wears your hand.

The Taxis' Song

the grannies they sit in taxis
the coloured boy with the coloured eyes
screams seapoint-seepunt in syncopation
grim lips tight coats against sea-cold
town-cold morning traffic to work

pass the tree-rand on
pass the tree-rand on
pass the tree-rand on

hello tannie
goeie-môre auntie
howzit lady with the apron on
we goin to work with the apron on

close you big thighs grannie
move you big ass auntie
squeeze you big breast tannie

anotha customer has come along
anotha lady she is gettin on

pass the tree-rand on
pass the tree-rand on
pass the tree-rand on

hold you feet still grannie
keep you purse now tannie
know you place neow auntie
the bumpy road it bumps us along

the morning-song the traffic-jams
the coloured boy's money in his right hand

keep you head neow grannie
see you eyes straight tannie
know you work now auntie

you stop just neow is comin along

and we be back to see you so long

in the ys-cold sea-koud stad where you born

pass the tree-rand on
pass the tree-rand on
pass the tree-rand on

Post-Colony: Do Not Love Freedom

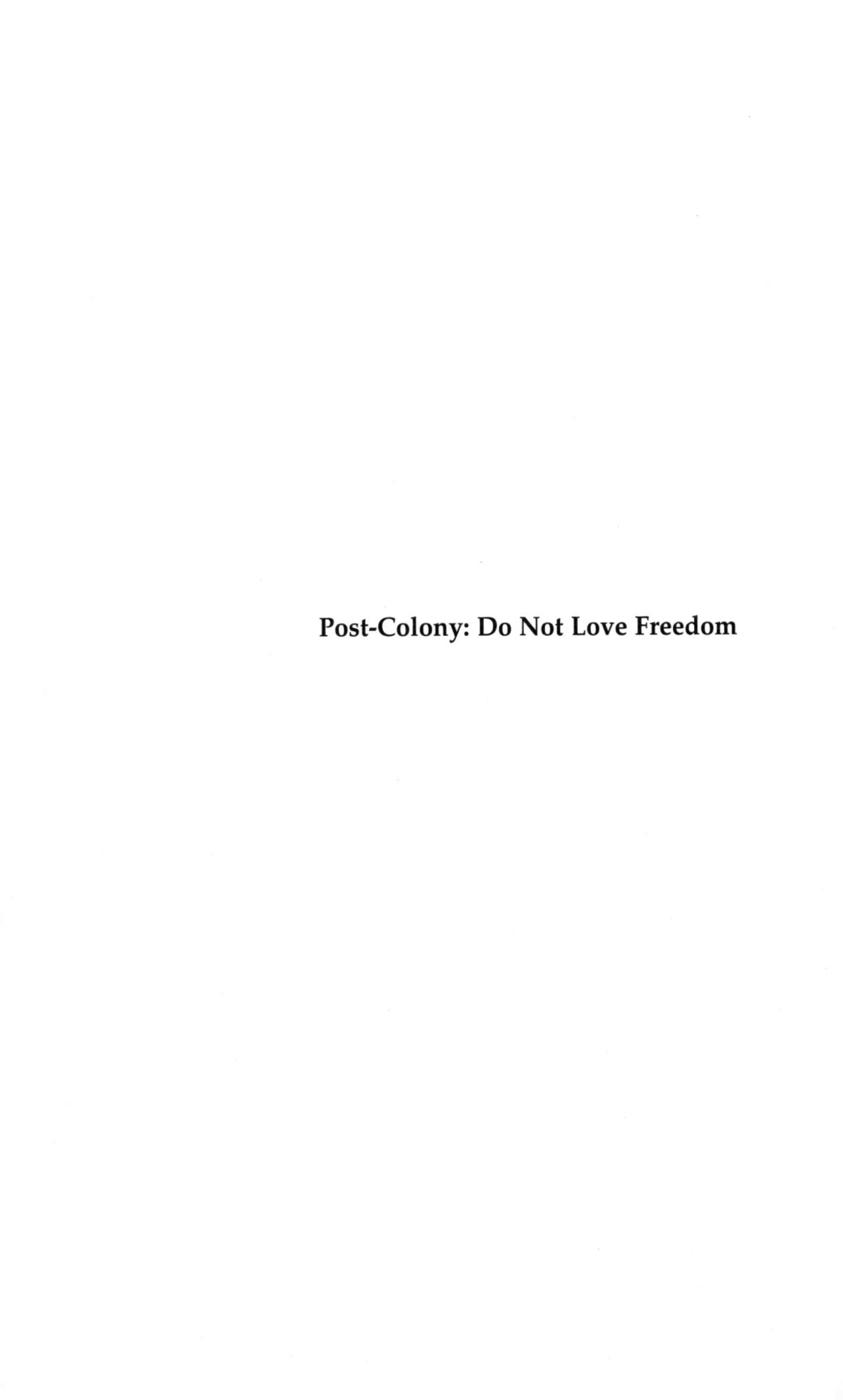

Do Not Love Freedom

Do not love freedom so much,
nor demand magic in your life.

The beauty of the world inspires such things,
lower your eyes and desire little,
like an ox bowed and stabled for the night.

Be careful, do not admire butterflies too much!
Do not love freedom,
so absolute, so graceful and so short-lived.

be a thorn tree
it lives for a thousand years without life
it can withstand the dryness of sand
the silence of the clouds

Be careful of green landscapes and mythologies.
Dragons and unicorns and knights and princesses
should be kept from the hearts of children;
children grow into bitter men and women.

be a tortoise that lives
lives of men beyond count
lay your eggs, seek the sea
and vanish without sound

Be grateful
for that small kindness
of a gentle wind on a blade of grass;
to live only enough to keep despair,
the twin in shadow, from leaning too close
to breathe on your brow at night.

It keeps women from touching rings of promise
with a hurt and resentful hand;
it keeps men from cursing a droughted land,
from leaving the women they once loved.

be a desert frog

bury yourself in the cool earth
and sleep as if dead
for twenty years you can bear
the lack of rain
imprisoned in the ground

No one knows the consequences of death,
but, I know the pain of loss.

Do not love so much,
my friend, do not love so much!

Mortar and Steel

They ask us to die for the things we least understand:
vague phrases that inspire our leap from the ship
the weight of fingertips on metal triggered . . .
not knowing that human minds are *not* like concrete buildings.

No wonder the scientists of ages past sought to prove our souls;
how do you rebuild what was not made with mortar and steel?

When I stood in Christchurch among dead kings and virginal saints
and touched the floors inlaid with mortal bodies
I heard a music from much further than I had come;
where, too, kings had buried what they loved.

What could I do but kneel?
Even an atheist is moved by a sacred place.

It was not to protect the marble that they wanted us unshod.
no, I will never forget it!
The cold white of it, my feet remember—
I grew out of that structure
as surely as if they had built me within it.

I could feel the centuries as I stood,
could trace the beauty with my lips
pressed hard on the mica, ivory . . .
I needed no Bishop to tell me its worth!

Can I gain mastery (over a thing) if I name it?

Despite the juxtapositions of heat with cold:
white marble with boldly hewn stone
a rosy dome with grey vaulted ceilings
the warmth with the wet, I was moved beyond moving.

Gracious Frideswyde, Beloved Arjumand
in each and every land I have been . . . *sanctus spiritus mundi,*
thunia and *zentheghee* . . . not the least of which:
the sand paintings lifted by the winds of the world in reverent song
the springbok dancing in the Fynbos

skies of trees and oceans like land to our feet.

Tell me then (must I ask it?). Writing has been dangerous
in any age the weight of spies and civil servants and poets
and painters and doctors and philosophers and believers
slow my lips to say it to whom shall I say it?
Dem r' murderer, killa.

Immigrant's Tempest

Immigrant with frowsy hair
and the shake in his dark arm
is remembering a war somewhere
somewhere more vivid than here.

The pale burgundy of the table's
creamy nicked edge feels his
drumming fingers poised for f/l/ight
in the Toronto-trapped coffee-time.

He's stolen a dollar-forty from his daughter's
plastic piggy bank, when in better days,
cheque-in-the-mail days, he's laughed
and put his change in, a moment of bliss—

Today is merely escape, been here for hours.
His hooded wife wouldn't dare fold arms
raise high those arches of brows,
her concern is to conceal from the children

his fear.

If he could say it (he certainly wouldn't in English),
he would say it like the poets of his land:
home is where green fronds burst with green
obliterate the eye, massacre it with colour.

Neon is light only to sightless fish;
the sign offends and irritates, soups/salads
he cannot afford
the last of the milk too is borrowed.

He laughs, squirming with the joke,
the tale to tell to no one . . . here
at the airport, cousins and relations
children in their best squealing—

the last goodbye for the rainbow land
a good joke, the kind of joke you tell only once

in a lifetime. The government wants to help,
the translator says, immigrant services

with the bureaucratic shrug, unsettled by his
emotion and rhythmic hands, the pain unintended.
I want to work, give me work, he pleads,
the officer's complacent face a mask he'd like to break.

His clothes unwashed for a month, though his wife
has become a washing machine in the tub.
Hating his children for the expense of the diapers
food pushed about in the vastness of the plate.

Sometimes he turns off the tv—
KFC families sitting down to a meal of dead meat,
they drive him crazy.
Hey, give me something to eat!

He's a Canadian Caliban, dreaming of prosperity,
waking to find his life usurped; a Gonzalo
in a storm of storms, wanting the right
if death is to take him, to not have to die in the sea.

He looks around, knowing he looks crazy;
his empty cup staring at him emptily.
Brushing his clothes of ash and stains
walking to the only exit that remains

he recalls:

Sudan, Eritrea, Rwanda.
Desert lands with living coupling sand
showering skies of baby-blue eyes
postcard crispness of screaming green

and
when he cries
it's the colour he remembers
of the homeland that is no longer his to claim.

My Love Is Faithful
(A poem for my father)

My Dad still dreams like an immigrant.
Still telling the story of an uncle in Jordan
put on a plane for being too drunk
too categorically in love with a Muslim girl;
no time for packin' up, politely fateful,
from roaringly poetic to suddenly in flight.

Now there was a King, he says,
savouring those words like Lazarus had just
walked out of his tomb and proved him right.
Hussein, who treated his humbler servants
from other holy lands just fine.

My Dad is an ambitious man
and for this they oughta write him up in the papers;
how he walked the barren streets of colder than thou
Canada for two months before the Gov made this village
boy a clerk for five bucks an hour in the otherwise
coke-filled, bull-roided eighties.
And the naughty pre-cougar cougar secretaries
blew smoke in his face, on his cheap impeccable suit
(that made me proud of him like a Captain Kirk
of new broadloomed worlds), and said he'd never rise higher
than a shorthand writer of other people's words.

Boy, did he prove that he wouldn't be defeated
by their second-hand lung cancer and furniture
begotten by the roadside of Toronto streets,
as he sits in his gothic living room fit for an audition
with a Victorian Queen . . . what might she ask him to sing?

How he raised us to be better than those sluggards
in the schoolyard still slugging away in my dreams.
A manager! He says, and that's just where you'll begin!
(A civil servant's golden ticket I long to fling in).
Ha-ha, for three cents a word for a new poesy, what worlds
could I afford to encounter otherwise?
All art is past-time in an immigrant's mind.

Like the hothouse I want to build for him in retirement,

hot-hot fire-tough desert flowers under plastic drapes,
while I fiddlely-diddle with these words (more poison-tipped
lace than unfolding pleasure), I grow man-eating rhythms of discontent
in the pale lightenment of spring, dreading the call to the Kafkaian-coffin
of this new achievement.
Suddenly, pressing for time.

Frugalist of dispassionate French to be mine;
where the women will come and go
speaking of the broken photocopier.
No Duras among them to demand
an understanding of the death of peaches
while I kill my pencils with fury waiting for the bored clock
to let-my-people-go.

Father mine, you are a hero of survival, from dusty goats
and washing in buckets to water from a sprinkler etching
it's sound of living surviving grass sounding tch-tch . . .
You have made me and bureaucratic policy proud.
Indeed, you are not a liar that any lie can be told about:

you are a statistic.

Not like any other dog-and-pony show,
 I live you . . .
 I admire you . . .
 and for this reason, I am un-inalienably unfair to you.

Gone are the poems where I wear your suit and smoke in the playground,
I take on your suit, and- put- the- poetry- down.

Father, there is no dissonance between us,
you know well of who I am;
you have never spoken of the world other than it is.
It is only the academic training and imagination
you wished for me that kills it.

And I
am the child of the murder that you have always planned.
(Sing for me, like the bravados of this land . . . my love was always faithful).

The Final Menagerie

I passed through a paper village under glass
where the explorers first found
silence and taught it to speak
. . . killing sand without mercy
            —Richard Shelton, *The Tattooed Desert*

I had not learned to ride a bicycle,
so I chopped through Jungles
careless of medicines and disease,
wrists and ankles threatening to dissolve
in my unease, hoping to change the meaning
of time, while there was still growing grass.
I hurried in a way that was not fast
'till technology caught me on a bus,
my tongue in the rear, my silence in first class—
I passed through a paper village under glass.

Free from the infection of open air
Museums squatting everywhere
birthing order and history prolifically.
Outside, forests budding light bulbs to appease
the rivers that have been damned.
Mountains with holes gaping round,
I spray-paint my words on every sound
but I speak no language believed
so I bury it under the ground
where the explorers first found

they didn't want to return home.
Spearing the tropics with economy,
they killed the Eden they tried to conceive.
They brought me paper that said
elephants could not cross imaginary lines
or the birds reach certain heights.
There is no antidote to sedentary imagination.
Though I wept on the deserts and blew breath
to dry the floods, it was not the meek
who held the silence and taught it to speak—

it was the Naturalist. His nets like weapons
stalking the air, extinguishing the ground;
what was not lost, he said he had found.
But brother, breathless I cry, you are no man,
you are a butterfly . . . across the eons, there is no reply.
The wind has stopped, the earth stands tersely,
like a pinned insect flailing bound—
a sinking ark drowning its final menagerie.
In drinking the world, we have become more thirsty;
we are compulsive gardeners *killing sand without mercy.*

An English Landscape

No mirror can show an image to break her
to break the visions already present in her eyes
webs for her are not about time, nor entrapment.

She is thinking of paper-wet skin.

Scraps of ideas,
like swans in a lake,
an English landscape,
arrange themselves;
ruffian children holding hands
to make a fence
dressed as vermillion pages.

But that is home, why come?

Ordered already by an esthetic
which she understands but does not interpolate
so like trees, rocks, dark shadings
are the descriptive thoughts and feelings.

And so she lists
as though touring the Alps,
the Lake District,
touring her own loves,
her own ordered esthetics.

Middle ground, a lake of reflection
the mirror that separates, sets apart
to exclude and absent.

Her mind is a suitcase,
a mouth without meaning;
her honey-moon a post-card
everyone visits in the mail.

An icarus of sight
the ethereal mountains
relegated to a high sky,

an expanse of air, there— is terror!

The sublime precipice,
sprung cities of the world at her feet,
spreading across the desert, disused, diseased.

She expels
an order, a placement of the horizon
(it's not linear, but a spatial argument).

I'm on vacation, she says,
to draw an elongated labia,
poke a lion in the chest,
and perhaps stand on its head.

To dis-empower with metonymic symbols
like Beagles chasing giraffes in a savannah,
a slave strung up like game,

she's climbed a mountain
only to find a descent.

But that is the foreign place, why call it home?

II

Tell me, if you travel,
how many words will you take with you
for the unknown object?

When a firecracker is fire from heaven
and a freak migration of locusts a plague,
what lurks in organic fruits,
what secret DNAs—

signs, symbols, icons, expanding
dialectics and associations.

What is unnatural in nature?

A fetus fossilized in a uterus,
a 250 year old tortoise committing suicide
over the edge of a garrison wall,
an ancient bird aroused by a flower's scent,
a rhinoceros completely in love with a man.

How does one order anomalies?

III

receding circle in every square
a ratio of bones
a nautilus spiral
phi

animals
who bury their prey
touch bones of their dead
suckle human babes

we

taste iron in mouths
caress plastic with tongues
enliven porcelain with blood

how can we say
nature is where we are not?

In-Celestial Beginnings

The concrete box,
the new age home;
a capitalist salute
to the nuclear family,
The nuclear factory next door.

In-celestial beginnings,
how did we climb the trees;
spawned from the seas,
Angled above the clouds.

Babylon—the gay cafe,
Corporate Biblical Traditions;
We are architects, technicians, engineers:
International icons of evolution.

In-celestial endings,
Of diversity—insofar as the commercials
allow it,
God-given right to T.V.
Water-proofed diggers of the
fruits of the sea.

Scum—pond—water's—edge

Puzzletry

Puzzletry

I

Night is screaming the sound of darkness; *Poetry*
the sound is drowning in my lungs.
The light whispers its desire—
no word can shape it!

II

In whose landscape are you loved; *The Picturesque*
who carves your dreams in living flesh?

Who dares to lie with you
in those fields opaque and green?

III

Light is a garland to dark rooms, *The Activist*
to the heady scent of flight;
so far I have committed no crimes,
shorn no skin with tears.

IV

Your tears are like razorblades; *The Lover*
I cannot stand the bleeding of your cheeks.

You say you would like to make a book of my skin
so that you can watch me open—

whose nightmare are you?

Being Brave

Bleeding Coal

a dark, dark tunnel:
like a wreck we die to the very core,
as if drowning at the heart
or collapsing inwards from skin to soul.
    —Pablo Neruda, *Death Alone*

The rain lies on the street abed;
the rain lies dead on the street
—or perhaps it is merely abed:
sheets falling, lights out,
the thunder calling.
In the skies, a breathing funnel.

Linking words like chain-mail
the poet is armed to the grave,
but the hard-cast adjectives escape in the runnel
where imagination wanders in *a dark, dark, tunnel:*

we cannot rescue it today.

There are places that are dungeons in the city,
Where the people are weeping in revelry;
they are all drunk on drinking grief.
Tonight all tales will be believed, the words
will break the air like the waves will murder the shore.

With open-mouth eyes, with shouted silent cries,
remembering empty callous rooms and arbitrary doors,
lying broken, lying naked on the floor
like a wreck we die to the very core.

A contagion, the stories infect like flame
and Fire is the sound of a hungry child
screaming in our ears for our eyes.
We would attack the air if we could see it, catch it.

The poet is lost in the syntax,
her metaphors are dead bodies pulled in a cart
away—the departure cannot be listened for,

she is imagining the invisible, impossible . . .

Have they killed us, taken our souls apart?
We cannot breathe *as if drowning at the heart.*

But the reign will not stop.
Evil thunders ordinarily for us;
we are an international community of violence,
multi-lingual in torture, cross-culturally catastrophic,
we are all children weeping in horror—

we are rivers bleeding coal.

Night will not complete itself now;
there are too many voices cut short, abrupt, lost, shut up.
The universe is closing in as it unfolds,
it is *collapsing inwards from skin to soul* . . .

Lisping Beneath the Cries

I've stayed in the front yard all my life,
I want a peek at the back
Where it's rough and untended and hungry weed grows.
A girl gets sick of a rose.
    —Gwendolyn Brooks, *a song in the front yard*

Help lift half the sky;
hungry hands get tired, it shows.
Imaginative limbs immobile in poverty,
stingy minds forget how to dream.
I have harassed too many hopes;
I have clutched my worn and wilted screams.
Held in my arms the child of strife,
the suckling stone: `it will all get better you know.'
As though my feet were suppliant to a knife,
I've stayed in the front yard all my life . . .

Where I am a statue to idle eyes,
an open mouth to empty pockets,
a worn cause to weary angels,
the twentieth prisoner in a ten-man cell.
Sorry, is coldly thrown up by manicured mouths,
(they are afraid that I will attack)
fling my flagrant cries away,
unwrap suicide from my dreams . . .
The front yard is a dying garden patch;
I'm hoping for green, *I want a peek at the back.*

I would like to see past the lack
of untended trees, where wealth will not hire a gardener,
to risk the barrenness of crumpled brown leaves,
to step on the cracks where rain never seeps.
It's not enough to live and breathe,
to die and be buried in sleek mud furrows.
I want to remember what I did not know;
I want hands to speak, laughter to hold.
I would like to tiptoe where it does not snow,
where it's rough and untended and hungry weed grows.

I will not say I was denied, I will not speak the words,
lost, forgotten, the marginal subaltern.
Although the beak of oppression crows;
although my wrists are stiff in leather woes;
although there is stench in my fragrant nose;
I shall take the knife from my feet and pry
the slates of every boarded back door.
And, when poetry lisps behind each mournful cry,
I need not hold the sky anymore. I think it shows,
when you can have the briar, *a girl gets sick of a rose.*

Being Brave
for K Proulz

Failing all else I'll choose to love you.
I'll remember the night that we didn't sleep;
how you held my hand as I stepped onto the boat
into your arms below deck
merely to sleep, you said.

But I know how you touched my prone body,
prone to disasters and fat retention
always always to male attention.
While I shifted, half-lidded gaze,
peaking at penetration, the dying groan
of concentration.

Yes, you punctured your promise
like all good boys do sometimes,
always always with me.
But those tears in the corners
of the dock are really sea-water drops,
I said.

I'm sorry sorry sorry, you said
as though repetition were retraction.
I didn't mean . . . What did your hands mean?
And what can I tell you about the moment
I decided to be brave?

I've got suntanned legs, I've got pictures of the sea . . .

I've got collections from the days of courage.
No, you didn't mistake my desire,
all sleeping beauties must be woken
with intercourse like interrogation:
unsheathed bequeathed spermal reeds
growing straight, waving in our green fields.

So, you had it. My softness swollen around you
arousing you. How you turned my head
held hard in your masculine hands

because one pinkness was not enough.

How horrified you would be,
like all good boys are!

I know desire.

Can you believe, despite the bitter women,
despite the warning warring women,
that I trusted you to promise me safety in sleep?
I am not a good girl. I left home. I let boys slip
through my dreams into my panties

I've got suntanned legs.

So I've decided to love you after the fact.
Because if I pretend that you were the prince
struggling with the wilderness outside my castle
struggling to set me free the only heroic way
you could, men can, then I will be the happy
princess of a fairy tale.

No Mariana wishing for my death
I will continue to be everyday everyboy's
reality girl, flirting hair, and slipshod underwear
from Bangkok to Berlin, perfume on my skin,
open-toed shoes, open-spread legs,
willing always always to be misled.

I've got pictures of the sea.

And you would claim
that you never wanted this for me.
For you are that nice man next door
with a cheerleader girlfriend, homecoming
queen date, cookie-baking, missionary-poisoned
wife . . . that we all long to be.

But I know desire.

Provoking Sympathy

On May 13, 1985 Wilson Goode, Philadelphia's first Black mayor, authorized the bombing of 6221 Osage Avenue after the complaints of neighbours, also Black, about the Afrocentric back-to-nature group headquartered there and calling itself Move. All the members of the group wore dreadlocks and had taken the surname Africa. In the bombing eleven people, including children, were killed and sixty-one homes in the neighbourhood were destroyed.

she cried as the child stood
hesitant in the last clear sky
he would ever see the last
before the whirling blades the whirling smoke
    —Lucille Clifton, move

our bones do not all dance
though the sun shine on this earth
we are taut at the seams
of our crippled human skin

he ordered death by falling
skies which he stared up at, food
ignored, tight held anxious hands
tight held eyes wondering at flight

hands over her eyes like a hood
she cried as the child stood
listless stranded the open space
not far away the neighbours moved

he did not know to hesitate
the ground seemed so far away
an order gained in simple haste
he moved his thumb awry

watching their petition replied
they heard the bomb in sudden outcry
hesitant in the last clear sky
before the movement carried them away

right is black and white

but that night that day
was only the sound of grey
the world lost its colour

where there were houses a waste
remained a fence surrounded
the bodies in scraps the faces
undecided on the final newscast

he would ever see the last
arid shamed lie he would offer
for every question accusation
he brushed the words away

the dead were hidden in their graves
the people packed and moved away
the sun may shine the darkness choke
but difference in our fragile minds remains

we can leave each place of fire
we can move refuse to hesitate
but whose sympathy can we provoke
before the whirling blades the whirling smoke

The Lover

The Only Garden
for RGC

There were days when I thought
I could feed you in the desert
from my own body

cool milk like spring water
breasts swelling for your thirst
to me that was love.

Like that man who sent
parts of his body to his beloved
dying as he is cherished.

In the sunlight, which rippled me golden,
I opened the gate
to the only garden I knew.

For you I gave up unicorns
fought dragons
forgave all past hurts

held my tongue.
For you, I became myself anew.
To me you were all magical things:

I knighted you Lancelot,
I blessed you Gabriel,
I crowned you Lion-hearted . . . Richard

For you I believed all good
endured all evil
gave up hope for reality.

Like mystics entranced
we breathed the same breath in sleep.

Truly I died when you left me
a woman who had never before
known humility.

Using words like weapons you cut me
like a butcher with a taste for the blood of dead things—
a lover with a penchant for murder.

You are a Catholic without belief in grace
a gardener with a hatred for growing things
a post-lapsarian world without redemption.

How could you leave me to the arms of others?

I wrapped my wrists in ropes
tied them together to bedposts
for wanting to touch you;

I moved far away for the desire to see you;
I stopped breathing for wanting to live without you.
But even if I cut off my ears
I would still hear every grain of your voice.

I cannot punish myself for every moment
I did not cherish you;
I cherished them all—even the terrifying nights

when we wept in each other's arms,
for your madness, for my frailty,
for your anger and my infinite desire.

When other men kiss me,
I feel only pressure against my lips;
when they tell me I am beautiful

I know I would disfigure myself
if it pleased your eye.
It has made me ill inside, this love.

I am a waning moon
a red and dying sun
a barren and infertile earth.

What should I do now?
I shall never see unicorns again

the carcasses of dragons litter my floor

the garden is rent and torn
the stone walls forever broken
the heroes tired and olden.

No man who lies in my bed can make it less empty
no love burn more;
I can call no kiss a kiss that does not leave your lips.

Your hatred has scorched my flesh;
my skin is black, obscenely
red flesh revealed through the cracks.

I damage myself in my dreams for your eyes;
I imagine knives at my throat, in my breast
your hands hard on the handle.

I have no numbness, every moment
I live you again, on my knees—
Once I was a woman who did not know humility.

Do you deserve this strange worship
or I this unsavory defeat—
are you not only a man?

(It was your hands which confused me,
I could not bear their complexity
their impossibility.)

But I am waking from my sleep;
I cannot let you steal the small living
I have left inside me.

Let me, let you go.

Fight The Air

You say you don't believe in cultural idioms.

Go to sleep,
I'm not that interesting anyway!

We know what happens to the messengers,
face up, hair streaming, Ophelia—
you don't believe in archetypes either.

I cannot fight you on any battleground;
how do you fight the air?

Except to encase in glass . . .
(I could watch you invisible
for hours, you said—if I had eyes).

You don't believe people can
see things that aren't there,
But what if they are and I've
just blinded you with my tongue?

It was simple,
you choked on catastrophe
and I removed your retina.

So, now we are twins,
You the dead, me the unliving

It's okay,
cruelty is easier to understand
than if I loved you.

If I loved you,
you would be encased in stone
and I would have taken more
than just your eyes.

Caught in the Cracks

Out-worn heart, in a time out-worn,
Come clear of the nets of wrong and right;
Laugh heart, again, in the gray twilight,
Sigh, heart, again, in the dew of the morn.
      —WB Yeats, *Into the Twilight*

She held her skin against brazen wind
tasting cold lips and brittle fingers;
behind, the moon with meagre grin
leaned memory barren before her.
The earth seemed to tilt and tip with scorn;
her feet were brave but balance shorn.
In the rain her eyes were mild
when the sunlight came like a troubled child,
she touched my sleeve, a lover forlorn,
with an *out-worn heart, in a time out-worn.*

I'm caught! she cried, I've lost the sea!
How can I live with no will to breathe?
I'm drowning on land; I'm choking on air;
I'm hungry for comfort, but the cupboard's bare;
I see no monsters, but I'm blind with fright;
I have a sword, but no battle to fight;
I listen for music, but I hear no song;
the well is full, but my thirst is gone.
Listen, I said, with reason there comes sight—
come clear of the nets of wrong and right!

No lie can bind you, no liar convince,
no skein surrounds you, no hook pulling in.
Love is no judge, no jury, no jail;
it cannot test you, nor can you fail.
It is no god with celestial light,
no bird of truth at unreachable height.
Touch your arms, they're bare and clean;
hold your body, it's strong and lean.
Dance and loose love's sour bite;
laugh heart, again, in the gray twilight.

Give no spectre a fearful gaze;
lose yourself in no demon's maze.
For night is a blanket to torment's frost;
stars a lantern to hope you've lost.
Listen! For sleep is winding its horn,
and the moon dreams it's been reborn.
The dance of life steps strongly still;
and joy more worthy than agony's will.
Come, my friend, from sorrow be torn,
sing, *heart, again, in the dew of the morn.*

Secondary Texts

There is a picture of us,
six years after the fact (or delusion)
of our falling in love;
in the days of the headiness
of the suppressed desire underneath
all those placid words,
those long dinners with complex and foreign foods.

(Which I now know to make in minutes
standing at the kitchen counter to eat
having found premade sauces and the like
to speed-up the seductive process
feeding meat-pieces to my cats
their sensitive stomachs resulting in less than sexy
wind-broken conclusions.)

Those long nights standing with vintage drinks
by some great body of water
vaguely broken-sentence speaking . . .
Until that night six years later
arguing with you over another dinner
(graduating to meatless complexities
of eggplant sauces and many-dairy, lentil-type soup),
this time, a fluffy love-slut dog to caress.

When suddenly we were framed.
Our intercourse (not to be mistaken
as the main course—flaccid mushrooms),
disguised as discourse was trapped on film.
Our bellies round, the evidence of our hunger
appeased, the plates wiped empty, littering
the space between us, the pots.

(Later, after hours of standing by an ocean
spraying it with laughter, as it splayed
its watery legs over us, we made love (or illusion);
but really, it was just a physiological conversation.

Confused by the fucking that was really talking

(especially after the finger swirls of cape-brandy-pudding
putting into each other's mouths),
I wandered home to find
the picture taken by our anonymous dinner guest.

Six years after the fact
a picture which completely encapsulated us:
your arm raised in defense of your closed eyes
and open lips while I (obviously not bewitched)
stared disgustedly taken aback
(the slut-dog happily in my lap),
electric eyes shooting neon signs.

I showed you this tableau
(after dessert, some yogurt-honey drizzled fruit thing),
and you laughed in your defense.

You've always looked at me this way, you said.
And I lost my breath and wished for a burger
having remembered that we had only made love once,
understood for the first time why that was.

After years of fearing that you might guess that I loved you
(lest your appetite for me be appeased),
I had made it impossible for you to love me.
Still, what never fails to amaze me
is that you didn't tell me from the first.

Now, an eternity (and miles) away
I take up smoking and don't much
notice my hunger any more.

Lindy's Moon

I first saw you barefoot, long-haired, dancing boy;
at once, your beauty like a young girl's innocence,
the sublime in human form,
an ordered landscape speaking of disarray—
literally one moon ago when
the moon was bright and lonely in the sky.

Because I have a man's courage and a poet's imagination,
I crossed the space between us
the way science fiction and physics claim time folds:
I took a step to your side, I crossed a mile.
Holding you before you touched me
I held you in my eyes.

You claim the moon made you offer the greenhouse:
the garden in the heart of the country
the generosity of scarred skin
the sweetness of a recently murdered love.

But I wanted to tell you about the trees like dragons
holding council against the wind;
I wanted to show you the forest surrounding us
in the glass bedroom, where the wild flowers pressed
close like our warm and naked words.

And you came to me for comfort again
after the long trip running from that lonely moon
which shone its light reaching across the lake
skipping through leaves and branches
pushing across the waves in the harbour
needing us in the coal darkness.

I offered my arms then to your curling form,
your straying hair, your nomadic legs.

In my restive sleep and fearsome dreams
where sickness has gripped my rebellious body
and shadows come to reclaim me as companion
I saw the moon suddenly waver and recede;

I listened to you say that you would take the world
but only on its knees.

And knowing the fragility of time and my patience
the disintegration of my body and mind
how could I?—

Try to tie down a tumble weed
cage a bird, imprison sound
force you to make promises Lindy . . .

Then let it be all.

Life is temporary; can my friends condemn me—
for dancing by the ocean, for kissing your lips,
for hearing the music humming from your skin?
For now I hear the music humming from your skin.

Sunshine Dreams and Constellation Plans

I have dissolved into the present;
I can no longer remember my sunshine dreams
and constellation plans.

I know I had them; I have postcards.
But reaching out to touch the memory
is like trying to script a voice.

I loved. I know, from the bank statements
and credit card bills, and lacy lingerie
I didn't have a year ago—I know from the dates.

There were mountains of various degree and kind
and oceans that never repeated the same word twice.
(I used to talk to that sea.)

And there was a boy, a man that once
held my hand, once desired, once feared me
in a place,
I remember his lips but not the taste of them.

Am I going mad?

I used to live in the past;
I could recall each scent and tea leaf.
In agony I would stop in the street
thinking it was the ocean, find myself kissing boys
waking upon the discovery that I *am* in the present.

You used to say: *do not long for me.*

But you never asked me to forget.
And here I am. Where are *you*?
Are you holding that ocean still somewhere.

Have you captured the moon
and the stars in your fingers,
the mountain in some loom.

Or are you also forgetful present-ly.

Do you remember when you
needed daily bodily reports
(as though I was an enemy beloved).

Am I too far away even for reconnaissance?

All I have left are portraits
without expression, with darkening
colours, what were those colours?

I swore I would never forget.
I knew that in leaving you
I would not even possess the pain

for long, that I so rightfully earned.
The scents, I catalogued, the simplest
sighs and laughter archived.

But my hunger and sleep and desire
are now, not yesterday, not even
a capitulation to some future.

Perhaps even the plants are wrong!
Was there bamboo?
What was yellow in the foliage?

Some kind of palm . . .
Cacti, do they remember my blood?
Streets, do they remember my step?

The Blue-eyed Dawn

Remember me when I am gone away,
Gone far away into the silent land;
When you can no more hold me by the hand,
Nor I half turn to go yet turning stay.
　　　—Christina Rossetti, *Remember*

With eyelashes dewy from sleep,
with caught curled fingers
holding the space you left,
I woke to a rugged blue-eyed dawn;
I woke bereft.
But faint broken capillaries lay
colouring my untethered wrists,
spreading like red tide stain
recalling the loss of night to day.
Remember me when I am gone away,

I screamed at the unlocked door,
the lifted latch, the hastily left note.
My arms did not hold you back
when the heated air cooled suddenly;
your desire had grown slack,
soft like sunshine, shapeless as sand,
the locus of a tornado turned astray.
You were once a wild storm, now calmed, delayed.
I have forgotten that the universe is grand.
I've gone far away into the silent land,

where I breathe bitterness like barbs;
in a drought of love,
I swallow weariness like brine.
I will the strayed fragments of the moment
 perfect past—to remember me . . .
to return where now alone I stand
in the stillness of your wake,
chasing your scent in this unsettled space.
Still, I recall your touch like a brand
when you can no more hold me by the hand.

I evoked you once from dormant dreams,
from desires birthed in quiet sleep.
So, I lay with eyelids shut,
unsteady in my conjurors spell,
touching my bruises rough,
longing to seize you without delay.
I hope the dusk will descend again
to avenge your memory with footsteps
at my door and your absence betray,
Nor I half-turn to go, yet turning stay.

Give Way

Our love is conflicted like the Middle East.
We both make outrageous claims
neither can support or deny.

We do it in public places
with microphones
and a cabinet of swag supporters.

(It's no secret we wish each other ill),
each offence recounted and spread about:
sides are taken, people die.

Our accusations are home-made,
but lethal.

We cry well, but photograph badly.

You see me as a blur,
I see you as a wave.
We do not remember what the other looks like.

We don't play fair.
You invoke the kitchen god
and I condemn the back stoop.

I declare you cannot sit on the couch;
you swear I shall bath nevermore.
We are dirty and tired

but aflame with right-ness.
We cannot divorce or move out;
at any moment, you may give—an inch.

Acknowledgements

Once while at Six Nations Reserve I was given a piece of invaluable advice by a Metis man with sparkling eyes. I have often returned to his words for guidance. He said, "No matter what you decide to do with your life, go and learn from the best." I am glad to say that I have been guided and supported by better friends and mentors than I could ask for.

Thank you to my husband, Craig Laatz, and my incredible family for their unwavering belief in my abilities and the love they surround me with. It would take a book to praise you all adequately.

Nurjehan Aziz and MG Vassanji, I admire you for the voices you bring to life and for making this whole process so thoroughly enjoyable.

John Coetzee, I owe you an enduring debt of gratitude for your incredible patience, kindness, and incisive feedback. Your long-term support of my work has prompted an evolution in my writing and taught me to expect more of myself. An extraordinary writer, academic, and mentor—you live where words live.

To my special readers, John K Noyes, Sabine Milz, and Pieter Joubert, over the past decade you have provided unflinching praise, courageous criticism, and friendship. Thank you.

I am deeply grateful to have been mentored by these phenomenally powerful women: Marg Wells, Cynthia Grant, Maroussia Ahmed, Wai-Lin Terry, and Althea Prince. Also, Sylvia Bowerbank I miss you though you would not want me to.

Thanks to Hugh Hodge for significant editorial help on some of the poems in the South African section. Ben Williams, thank you for the gift of the line you sent me on a postcard: "The buildings were blinding like erected snow."

Thomas Cartwright, John Cartwright, Sam Sperry, and Bie Engelen, you have been a second family to me.

Thanks to the University of Cape Town and McMaster University for nurturing me as an academic and writer, especially: Harry Garuba, Noeleen Murray, Ferozah Jacobs, Peter Knox-Shaw, Jeffery Donaldson, Susie O'Brien, Daniel Coleman, Dannabang Kuwabong, Ruth Frager, and Peter Walmsley.

A special thanks to the artists and friends who have been a part of this book: Mayor David Miller, "Oh Susanna", Aidan Mason & Jorn Juul Anderson, Veronica Hyatt, Hal Swann, Jeff Davidson, Tiffany Martin, Frank Manfredi, Elizabeth Jackson, Kristen De Fillipis, Vivian Peachy, Maria Nunes, and others.

So many of my friends have been a huge support in my life and work: Jessica MacQueen, Graeme MacQueen, Grant McCracken, Brian Khan, Willem Simonis, Kathy Lim, Sheridan Manfredi, Ian Terry, Gessie Sterns, Adam Hayashi, Rachel Davies, Brian Bertrand, Sam Dizon, Amar Bhatia, Bojana Zizic, Mireille Troung, Eva Kloeve, Undine Kayser, Jyoti Narshi, Lauren Star, Ian van Biljon, Zebulon Vilakazi, Mary Seemane, Henri Yere, David Gault, Eric Lalonde, Graham Culverhouse, Andreas Lehman, Jilly Retson, Tugomir Williams, Abi Pugh, Doug James, Mr Howse, Michelle Madado, Patricia Barrotti, Jos E Humphrey, Meagen Procunier, Yvonne & Robert Laatz, and so many others.

Lastly, thank you to my readers for keeping poetry alive.